Night
on Ben Talaidh

Eunice Wilson

*The tragic accident on Ben Talaidh is unique in that it is
seldom an aircraft flies into a mountain without all being killed"*

*Dr Flora MacDonald,
recalling the night of the accident*

Brown & Whittaker
2005

ISBN 1904 353053

Cover illustration: *Plane in night sky* © Alastair Garvie

Brown & Whittaker Publishing
Tobermory PA75 6PR
www.brown-whittaker.co.uk

Set in Times New Roman and printed by Nevisprint, Fort William

Author's note

My own first contact with Mull was in my early teenage years when we were holidaying in Oban. Sitting on a bench on the front, watching the boat trips setting out for Craignure and MacBrayne's vessels going even further, we decided to go. But one day was not enough. We had to go again to see Staffa and Iona: there was too much magic to take in at one go. Years later, in Ireland, standing on the Giant's Causeway, I tried to visualise the bridge it must have created between the two coastlines where submarines once lurked under the sea, threatening all who ventured out. So to be given the job of finding the Dakota, tragic though it was, has been a fascinating search, bringing back a time when I was not much younger than the young men who lost their lives and many of the brave rescuers. There are many who will climb here who do not know what happened, many who are far too young, thank God, to realise the significance of the pieces of metal they may find. Please leave them be, where they lie. They are a Memorial to Freedom hardly won and at great cost. This must have been one of the most dramatic rescues of all time, impossible to imagine when the sun shines and the sea is calm. Sadly, and soon, only Ben Talaidh will remember and she is silent. I hope this story will fill that gap and bring more out from the island's memory.

Where the plane came down.
A fragment lying in the grass.

Acknowledgements

Most of the thanks must go to Olive Brown and Jean Whittaker who found a great deal of material already held on Mull and about people who remembered the crash or knew the facts of that dreadful night. From what they sent to me, based on material in the Mull Museum, I was able to locate more information at The National Archive (P.R.O.), to the staff of which must go thanks for locating obscure files. Without, on the other hand, the telephone calls and the personal stories received, an account of one of the RAF's tragic accidents could not have been put together.

Sgt Ian Erskine of Tobermory police and Miss Iona Whyte a schoolgirl who took the crash as her subject for a project made considerable contributions as did Bill Duffin, a knowledgeable fellow researcher and another Scot. Sergeant Neil Owen and David Howitt gave help with technical details. Most of all thank you to all the other people who, without a thought for themselves, rescued the survivors from what could have been even worse than it already was. Sqn Ldr Auchinvole's son, Alasdair, supplied photographs of his father. The mystery remains largely unsolved.

Illustrations

KK194

Towards the end of January 1945, Dakota KK194 took off from Dorval near Montreal in Canada. Although the weather was recorded by Dorval as "normal" – but cold – it seems to have deteriorated and was poor when they called at the Staging Post at Reykjavik to refuel. It is not known how long the crew stayed at the Iceland base hoping it would clear, which means that the departure from Canada could have been within the previous week. In Iceland, extremely bad weather in December and January had caused visibility to be reduced to 5-10 miles and to less than one mile in snow storms. It may have been prudent to wait and if the crew did this, it may account for the lack of departure times which are usually recorded meticulously to the minute. It was here that Flt Lt Derek Auchinvole, a Transatlantic Air Traffic Controller at Prestwick, joined the complement. Auchinvole had arrived at Prestwick on 1st August 1944 on the cessation of detachment which means he had returned from another job away from his base. The record does not say what this detachment might have been but it was presumably a ferry flight. On the 19th October he was posted to 86 Staging Post on Iceland and it is assumed that from here he picked up the Dakota on its way from Canada to Prestwick.

The next entry on TAC's records notes that on 1st February 1945 Dakota IV KK194 had crashed on the Isle of Mull on a delivery flight from Dorval in Canada to Prestwick. F/O Bishop 162502, the pilot, F/O H Ellis of 86 Staging Post on Iceland and Sqn Ldr A E Alderton, the Air Ministry Courier had been killed.

A Dakota sitting in snow on the tarmac at Prestwick, 1947

The Rescue

On the Isle of Mull that night the weather was the worst that anyone could remember. It was cold enough to freeze your eyes and ears and one man who had lived in Canada said it was worse even than a winter there. It comes dark early and quickly on Mull and at 6.30 on the evening of Thursday 1st February 1945, the cloud had come down and the quiet was intensified. It was what the RAF would call a 'clamp' of the highest order. Suddenly there was the dreadful but muffled noise of a crash near the summit of Ben Talaidh. From the sound of an aircraft flying low that had preceded the shock, everyone knew what it could be, though such things seldom happened here.

The aircraft struck the mountain obliquely at 2,300 feet, just below the summit. It slid down a further 500 feet and two of its occupants were thrown clear out into the snow. It came to rest in a highly precarious position where movement would have dislodged it to slide even further into a rocky gorge below, from which it would have been difficult to save anyone alive. As it was, one man got out and tried to go for help and flares were sent up.

Far below, people were not slow to respond to the summons of the distress flares. To a man, they scrambled up the precipitous slopes to rescue whoever was still alive. Flt Lt Derek B Auchinvole, recorded as a passenger, was the man who had got out and had already struggled away from the wreck, even though he was in great pain from a back injury. He crawled towards the two airmen who had been thrown out by the force of the crash. He found Flt Lt Basil Miller but could not lift him, so he dragged him back to where the fuselage of the aircraft offered some protection.

There was always the danger that the aircraft would burst into flames but he would have died if left exposed in the snow and wind. Miller wrote afterwards to Sir James Ross of the Air Ministry, that the Flight Lieutenant, who had been promoted to Squadron Leader later that year, had saved his life. Auchinvole then went to help the other victim, the pilot, Frank Bishop, who was badly injured but alive. He later died from his injuries. Then he stumbled down the hillside towards a light far below in the glen to look for assistance. Reaching it, he fainted, but not before he had told the people he found there in an ever-weakening voice, where the aircraft was. The account of Dr Flora MacDonald, the doctor in the second rescue party to be mobilised is given opposite.

Flight Lieutenant Derek Auchinvole

The glen at that time was peopled by shepherds Tom MacDonald at Kilbeg. The MacNeilages at Godhail. The Fishers at Rhasil & the MacDonalds better known as the Garov at Bentalla Cottage.

It is wonderful how trifles often come to matter very much in life. Mrs Fisher suffered badly from rheumatism & she always depended on her husband to put up the black out at night. Fisher had slipped that day & hurt his leg & did not feel like climbing on a chair. so he said Och leave it alone there'll be no one about on a night like this ...

As medicals we were among the first to be notified. I took on myself to ring up the minister Rev A D MacRae. Mrs Morrison Penmore's brother who was in Salen Manse. He came at once. Next day told me how glad he was I had told him as he would have hated to awaken next day & hear what had happened in the night without his knowledge.

Cars were little use. so vans & lorries were assembled & the men rushed around for spades & shovels ... The men had to stop & dig out the vehicles every now & then ...

The road stops at Godhail & thereafter there is only a track which was quite obscured by the deep snow. The going was pretty awful ...

Finally we heard the slapping crashing of the tail plane in the wind & finally reached them

Extracted highlights from Dr Flora's account of the rescue

Within half an hour of hearing the crash, George Beale, then aged 50, the owner of the Glenforsa estate, organised a search party from the Estate House. With Thomas MacDonald and John MacDougall, he was on his way up the glen. With the latter aged 54 and 64, none of them were young men.

It had been only a quarter of an hour since they had seen the distress signals. On the other side of a fragile suspension bridge, they found Flt Lt Auchinvole at Rhoail. Shocked and exhausted, he told them the exact location and they sent back MacDougall with his message to the police in Salen to get in touch with the RAF and to send a rescue party. MacDougall then had to go to his own croft to attend to his cattle and sheep, suffering in the storm, but he went back alone later on his own initiative to help.

Beale and MacDonald then went up the corrie, keeping to the east side and picking up Donald MacLean from Ben Talaidh Cottage on the way. At midnight, they reached the wreckage and the three injured men inside where Auchinvole had dragged them. They carried the other two into it for shelter, but one died soon afterwards. All around was the reek of fuel. It is not entirely clear what happened

The cottage and the modern footbridge at Rhaoil

next, but it seems likely that, unable to do more, Beale and MacDonald went back down the hill to make sure that MacDougall had got through and further help was on its way. MacLean may have been left with the casualties.

Down below, hot tea was busily being prepared for the rescuers, for the night was still black and the cold piercing, and Mrs Beale and Archibald Cattanach went down into Salen where Police Constable Hume had passed on the message and collected together two more parties. She rallied the rest of the women to prepare food, but there was no one who did not know what was expected of them.

Dr Flora MacDonald, Rev Alex MacRae, Archibald Cattanach, Donald Ross and William Walker were the next on the scene. Flt Lt Basil Miller was partially conscious when they arrived and he remembered them coming through the mist and the still falling snow, with the two local men who had guided the stretcher bearers to carry him down. Dr Flora had cut her leg in the rough climb and at one time had to be pulled out of waist deep icy water. She gave first aid to the injured and made them more comfortable while the others searched, without success, for the body of a man who had been thrown clear on impact.

Dr Flora MacDonald in 1956

The third rescue party from Glen Forsa was led by Dr Reginald MacDonald, who was 67, John Black, a motor driver and Dugald Carmichael who was 28. Their courage was unimaginable.

The second party had reached the aircraft at 2.15 on Friday morning and the third at 3.30. Still in the dark, since the full moon did not rise till 06.41, Thomas MacDonald and Donald Ross made another attempt to find the body that had been thrown clear. They tried to get up the slope to where it might lie. But it was steep and dangerous and in the darkness they failed, again, to find it. Nothing more could be done in the dark and if the man had been still alive at the time of the crash he was surely not so now in this exposure.

Up on the mountain, the sides of the corrie below the crashed aircraft were icily dangerous and any slight movement of the wreckage could cause it to slip further down, deep into the gorge.

It must be remembered that there were no helicopters then, no Search and Rescue Squadrons and none of the equipment which modern climbers take for granted. Nothing could come quickly enough. Snow and ice lay deep in the glen and up the track there were deep drifts into which a fall could be fatal. Alternate severe frosts and thaws had rendered every surface horribly treacherous. Even in the best of summer conditions the way up the glen was little more than a cart track and the river was in flood, its banks unstable.

A little after 4.00, a fourth party was on its way. Mrs Hume from the Police Station had telephoned Police Sergeant Barnaby in Tobermory and he asked the Naval authority urgently for a search party and stretchers. In less than half an hour, two officers and fifteen ratings were on their way. They were all volunteers and most of them without knowledge of the mountains. Neil MacKechnie who drove them as far as their vehicle could take them, went up the mountain with them, and Police Sergeant Barnaby with Constable McLeod led the party.

They had left Tobermory at 1.15 a.m. on icy roads on one of the darkest of winter nights. They had reached Salen (nine miles away) at 2.15. Two hours later they were at the MacLeans' cottage which became their base at the head of the Glen. Navy Lt Grumbridge and Surgeon Lt Belby, the fifteen ratings, the two policemen and Neil MacKechnie went up the east side of the corrie as the other parties had done. They could see nothing and were forced to return to the cottage at 6.30.

Cattanach had seen their lights from the aircraft and was astonished to see the naval party turn away. He and Walker went down to the cottage to guide them back. The naval men unused to this, were by now becoming exhausted and Cattanach, Walker and McLeod did most of the work. By the time it was light at 9.30 a.m. they were back on the scene with the stretchers and the navy men were appalled at what they saw. Constable McLeod took guard and responsibility for the personal property and the important official documents the aircraft was carrying. The dead body of Sqn Ldr A F Alderton was removed from the wreck and stretchers were prepared to take him and the injured down the mountainside.

At 11 a.m. when it was fully light, Cattanach, Walker and Ross made the climb successfully, recovered the body higher up and brought it down by sliding it over the edge with a rope. Undignified but essential. The Rev MacRae had insisted on going up with them and got half way but they made him go back, he was after all, not a mountaineer and was exhausted.

It was nearly mid-day when the naval volunteers got down with the stretchers, each party being guided by a shepherd. It was a night none of them would forget. They were met by an RAF party who took the injured men into Salen. There they were taken aboard an RN speedboat and moved into hospital in Oban. Mr Beale got back home about 7 p.m. utterly exhausted. Cattanach even worse, was in a state of complete physical collapse. The women who had been up all night making food and drinks for the rescue parties and bandages for the injured until all their supplies were gone, sat back, able to relax at last.

Port side of aircraft fin with remnants of rudder attached

Lives were saved that night by this display of enormous courage and endurance in appalling weather. There had been very serious risk to all the rescuers and it was remarkable that none of them was lost.

Clearing the wreckage

The Inquiry

On the 1st February, it was bluntly recorded at TAC (Transatlantic Control) RAF Prestwick that a Dakota IV KK194 had crashed on the Isle of Mull on a delivery flight from Dorval in Canada to Prestwick. F/O Bishop 162502, the pilot, F/O H. Ellis of 86 Staging Post on Iceland and Sqn Ldr A.E. Alderton, the Air Ministry Courier had been killed.

On the 5th a Court of Inquiry was assembled at Prestwick to enquire into the reasons for the flying accident though it was painfully obvious what they were – exceptionally bad weather in which the disorientated Dakota crew had flown into a mountain. It is all too probable that their descent was forced upon them as the aircraft became burdened with ice and the fact that the plane hit the mountain at a rising angle suggests that the pilot may have been trying to take avoiding action. For some reason, radar could not detect it, or the weighted plane could not rise or turn in time. It was not as though the Transport command pilot was inexperienced or that he was not accompanied by a Traffic Controller whose job it was to know the route from Iceland to Prestwick. Both had done flights like this before.

The President of the Inquiry was Sqn Ldr D.S.M. Scott AFC 45229 from the HQ Unit of 44 Group to which the aircraft belonged. He had taken over from 45 Group, with Flt Lt R H V Thomas 123947 of RAF Dundonald, as the Member of the Panel. In the records of an Inquiry there are more people than this involved, but the transcript is missing. Often there are photographs, but perhaps these were not possible because of the position of the wreckage and the weather conditions. More often than not, there are reports from the people who had last serviced the aircraft to determine its airworthiness, but again, distance and weather may have rendered these also impossible. Certainly, there are usually witnesses but as no-one actually saw the crash happen, though there were many rescuers, none could be called.

What there is, is contained in the station records of Prestwick in TNA file AIR 28/463. Yet there were passengers involved and there is nothing from the heroic Auchinvole. Two other crashes within a few days, are recorded at Prestwick in the Operations Record Book which may also have been due to the weather.

Either what the Dakota was carrying was so secret nothing more was recorded, or there is a simple answer – the results of the Inquiry have been lost. The latter is not unusual, not through a deliberate mislaying or a cover-up, but because the system of preserving documents is not infallible.

Prestwick's documentation – AIR28/653 – has no record of Flt Lt Auchinvole being given survival leave nor being sent to hospital after his ordeal, But surely, after rescuing other crew members, stumbling down an unfamiliar mountain with an injured back, he deserved and needed both. All we have is that in due course he was posted back to Prestwick from RAF Ossington, which was a training unit for traffic control officers and other personnel, There are many other nationalities in its postings-in and out listing in AIR28/606 but nothing for him.

There are several other classes of documents at the TNA which refer to crashes of all kinds. In none does Dakota KK194 appear.

Without wishing to stir up something seemingly mysterious which may be solved elsewhere, it suggests to the curious minded, that when at first the Air Ministry were reluctant to make the awards that they eventually did, could it have been that there was something to which they did not want to draw attention? Only time may tell. Life is more important than documents, but was there someone among the service rescuers who was detailed to find and bring down something else when the courier was found dead? After the injured and the bodies had been brought down, even the police would not have gone up alone again until the weather had subsided and become more calm. But someone would have had to go. In the meantime – ?

A visit was made to the scene, presumably as part of the Inquiry, but mainly to talk to the rescuers and others involved. It does not state if any of the visitors actually climbed to the wreckage. A letter in Air 2/6962 – which is still under restricted access – says there was some query about the body of Sqn Ldr A E Alderton, the Air Ministry courier, which was at first said to have been crushed under the aircraft. His brother telephoned the Air Ministry to say that his sister had received a letter saying the body was unmarked and he queried the difference. This may have been only to spare her feelings, as it is added in handwriting to the typed copy in the file. This was quite usual when injuries were severe, and it is unlikely there is anything sinister in this.

But there is some slight difference in the accounts of who was on board the aircraft and without the Inquiry report it is not possible to confirm who the personnel were. When an aircraft takes off, the date and time-up is logged, so are the names of the crew and passengers as well as its destination. F/O Frank Bishop was the pilot, who died from his severe injuries. Another man was thrown out of the aircraft when it first struck the mountain and was dead when the rescuers eventually found his body. The aircraft must have broken open for this to happen. This could have been Ellis, the navigator, though not named initially. Flt Lt Auchinvole's part in the rescue is well accounted for.

Unless more documentation is found relating to Reykyavik, there is no more to be found to clarify what we have, and to ascertain exactly who and what was on board KK194. This is not to say there is a mystery or something suppressed. A great deal of confidential mail and documents of all kinds were transported across the Atlantic to and from everywhere in WW2. It was the safest way for the Allies to keep in touch and in close co-operation. But it still leaves, as many documents do, a lot of questions and in Inquiries there are few without answers, for they are gone into in great detail and the RAF, as far as it is able, needs to determine exactly what happened. Their intention is to try to prevent it happening again – in the current phrase, to alert everyone to an "accident waiting to happen." Things are, thank God, much safer now, but weather, though it can be forecast and measures taken against it, cannot be controlled.

The MoD accident card for KK194 says that the results of the Inquiry lead them to believe that the wireless operator did not receive the messages correctly or interpreted them wrongly and says the aircraft descending at night through low cloud, uncertain of position, crashed into the mountain. It is sadly easy to blame dead men and as there is no Inquiry report, this is the final answer. To this author, it seems that both the pilot and crew were blamed for something beyond their control.

The mystery

The absence of records need not, in itself, be suspect. Documents do get lost, it is a human failing. But it leaves a suspicion their place. Like a big hole that cannot be filled in. There are plenty of unsinister possibilities, but there are no answers. Case unsolved.

Relevant page from Operational Record Book, Prestwick, AIR 28/463

Rescue of the Crew of a Royal Air Force aircraft
on Ben Talaidh, Island of Mull.

THE AIR COUNCIL desire to put on record their high appreciation of the gallant services rendered by the people of SALEN AND GLEN FORSA, when an aircraft of the Royal Air Force Transport Command, on the last stage of a journey from Canada, crashed near the summit of Ben Talaidh on the night of 1st February, 1945. The five surviving occupants of the aircraft were rescued & brought down to safety.

The weather conditions in the glen and on the mountain were the most severe in living memory. Snow & ice lay everywhere in the glen & up the mountain, with deep drifts, while the night itself was dark & there was intermittent snow & hail. Distress signals from the wrecked aircraft were seen in Glen Forsa & the organising of relief parties was at once begun. Successive parties went up at intervals throughout the night & completed the rescue work in conditions which taxed to the uttermost the physical strength & endurance of the rescuers. Whatever risk was required on the mountain side was taken & great courage and determination were shown by all.

Public recognition of these gallant services was given by His Majesty the King as follows—
Appointed a Member of the Order of the British Empire: Dr. Flora Livingstone MacDonald, M.B., Ch.B.
Awarded British Empire Medal: Mr. Archibald Cattanach. ❖ Mr. Donald Ross ❖ Mr. William Walker.
Awarded Commendation: Mr. George Robert Beale ❖ Mr. Thomas MacDonald ❖ Mr. Donald MacLean ❖
Dr. Reginald N. MacDonald, L.R.C.P. L.R.C.S. Ed. ❖ Mr. John MacDougall ❖ Rev. Alexander Duncan MacRae, M.A.
Letters of thanks for noteworthy assistance were sent to the following:
Mr. John Black · Mr. Dugald Carmichael · Mr. Neil MacKechnie · Mr. John MacQuarie · Mrs. Margaret Fisher ·
Mrs. Catherine MacLean · Mrs. Mary MacNeilage.

THE AIR COUNCIL also desire to record their gratitude for the outstanding help given by a party of officers & men of the ROYAL NAVY. They also record their thanks for help given by members of the County Police and by others not individually named.

THE AIR COUNCIL trust that for years to come this tribute to the gallantry of the rescuers will bear witness to the spirit of service and sacrifice which never failed the nation, at home or abroad, in these years of struggle for FREEDOM AND JUSTICE.

Air Ministry. London. October. 1945.   Permanent Under-Secretary of State for Air.

The Vellum,
Salen School

The Awards

Later that year, several awards were made to the people who had gone up in relays to help. It would seem from the letters in the file at the Public Record Office that there was at first some reluctance to make any awards, though there is no explanation of why this should be. The reason perhaps was that there had been many crashes and many rescues, and it could be that the powers-that-be had not heard the full and unique story. Or what was more likely, the RAF sites were still essentially secret and to publicise them when the war was not yet over, might attract new dangers from new enemies.

It cannot be that the Scottish Home Department in Edinburgh did not know by June 1945 what was proposed, for Sir James Stirling Ross KBE, CB had written from the Air Ministry in Whitehall in June telling the Department about the rescue by the people of Tobermory and Salen of the victims of the crashed Dakota. He suggested that an acknowledgement at least should be made.

The Department had received a recommendation from the Police and Fire Service for an award to be made to Sergeant George E Barnaby who was active in organising the search. But, they continue, it is unlikely that any award could be made. Why not? Had no one recommended anyone else? No doubt he deserved an award but after all, there were others, civilians, who were on the scene even before Barnaby could be alerted.

It was agreed it would be appreciated locally if Ross could send messages of appreciation as he had suggested, and framed letters would also be welcome. They did go so far as to suggest the village hall in Salen would be a suitable place to display the citation, though the Town Clerk had suggested the Post Office and that the Rev Alexander MacRae of the Manse would be the best person to consult as he was also the local County Councillor. There was no mention of the minister's personal appearance on the scene as part of the first volunteer party, nor his second climb to try to find the missing crewman.

Such are the distant ways of authority. It is rewarding in itself to see that someone caused them to change their minds. Item 26 3/6 in the local archive has a photograph of the group, the citation and an account of the presentation. It was held in Salen on 3rd Nov 1945 and was attended by at least 150 people including school children from Glen Forsa

Those present were:

Sir James Ross KBE, who presented the Tribute from the Air Ministry
The Chief Inspector of Police in Edinburgh
Major Duncan McCallum, MP for Argyll, represented the Secretary of State
Air Commodore L T Pankhurst CBE represented the C-in-C of Transport Command
Mr Peter Ferguson of Dunoon, Convenor of Argyll County Council & his wife
Chief Constable and Mrs Ross, Argyll Constabulary
Rev Mr and Mrs A D MacRae of the manse at Salen
Mr D Smith, Argyll County Clerk and his wife
Flying Officer Hewitt in charge of the RAF Guard of Honour from Prestwick.

IMPACT

REST

Auchinvole's route

Be
(T

Notes:
The point of impact can be identified by walking down the hill from the summit until the first small pieces of debris are found. The exact spot where the aeroplane finally came to rest can be identified from the photograph on page 11. The compass was found by a party in 1982 on its final bearing of 163° (Tomsleibhe Bothy Book entry). Adjusted for 13° mag. var. in 1945, this is 150° True – straight up Glen Forsa.

The place where Auchinvole crossed the river is conjectural. It has been assumed that he followed the valley bottom heading for the welcome light. Only at the last moment would he have realised that he was on the wrong side of the river, and waded across it, not knowing that there was a bridge downstream. This bridge was slightly upstream from the present bridge. The course of the river was altered in the 1960s but the concrete pillars from which the old bridge was suspended can still be seen either side of the dry river bed.

h Cottage
he bothy)

Rhaoil

Footbridge

The Night of 1st– 2nd February 1945

18.30	KK194 hits Ben Talaidh and slides 500 feet down the mountain
18.45	Flares seen
19.00	First rescue party (Beale) set off to investigate
24.00	First rescue party reach casualty
02.15	Second rescue party (Cattanach/Dr Flora MacDonald) reach casualty, followed by Third rescue party (Hume)
09.30	Fourth rescue party (Navy with stretchers) reach casualty
11.00	Last body recovered from crash site.

The Citations

M.B.E

Dr Flora MacDonald

B.E.M.

Archibald Cattanach

Donald Ross

William Walker

Commendations

George Robert Beale

Thomas MacDonald

Donald MacLean

Dr Reginald MacDonald

John MacDougall

Rev Alexander MacRae

Letters of Thanks

John Black

Dougal Carmichael

Neil MacKechnie

John MacQuarrie

Mrs Margaret Fisher

Mrs Catherine MacLean

Mrs Mary MacNeilage

Officers and men of the Navy at Tobermory

Argyll County Police.

There were lavish floral decorations in the village hall and the visitors were afterwards given a splendid lunch at Salen Hotel. An apology from the Secretary of State for his not being able to be present due to sickness was read by his representative Mr Kinnear. Afterwards, they sang "O God Our Help in Ages Past" and Rev MacRae pronounced the Benediction, followed by "God Save the King."

A copy of the vellum marking this amazing story of rescue was made and presented to each of them as well as a framed copy to be hung in the church at Salen. It now hangs in the entrance foyer of Salen School.

Archie Cattanach B.E.M.

Rev Alex MacRae

The Courier

It is rumoured that the aircraft was carrying important papers for the Middle East, and these may have been the reason for their being accompanied by the Air Ministry courier. Indeed Dorval was responsible for dispatching aircraft of all kinds all over the world and these are recorded in detail. Air 25/648 showing 45 Atlantic Transport Group at Dorval as being out of action due to bad weather and heavy snow, nevertheless lists that on 31 January three Dakotas were despatched for the Middle East and 34 to the UK.

Normally the police are the first on the scene of a crash and they, in turn, report what they find to the nearest RAF station who immediately send out a rescue team and prepare sick quarters and the morgue.

A curiosity still remains. Who was actually in the aircraft beyond the crew differs in various reports. The records of 45 Atlantic Transport Group at Dorval, seem to be the most reliable. They say the Captain and pilot was F/O Bishop, the navigator F/O T B M Alexander, the Wireless Operator W/O G Nicholls and five passengers. The latter are not listed by name but we know Flt Lt Auchinvole, not crew, was one because he was the one who pulled the others to relative safety and went for help. We also know that F/O Miller was another non-crew survivor, because later he went to thank Auchinvole for saving his life. Also there was Ellis and Anderton the courier, a total of eight.

The report continues that the Court of Inquiry was instituted by 44 Group. We have the entry in their Operational Record Book ORB that it was transferred to 45 Group, Prestwick, held there and with the names recorded of the two officers involved, but with no more. The Captain and two passengers were killed, the report continues, two crew seriously injured, one of whom was suffering from shock – Auchinvole? who was not crew – and two were dangerously ill, the other must have been Miller. It is difficult to understand whom they describe as passengers, Bishop, Alexander and Nicholls being crew

All the documents from Dorval are signed by the AOC, AVM R L Matrix, the officer commanding. But without the report from the court of inquiry it is difficult to verify the rest, and there is no hope now it will turn up.

Front aspect of
R-1830
Pratt & Whitney
twin wasp radial engine.

The Final Tally

The Casualties:

Sqn Ldr Archibald Ernest Alderton 73063 was the son of James and Elizabeth Annett Alderton and husband of Marjorie. He is buried at Brookwood Cemetery, South Croydon, Surrey. He was the Air Ministry courier and aged 45.

F/O Bishop VR 162502 is buried in Cardiff Western Cemetery Glamorgan in Section H Grave 1758

F/O Ellis 158646 was aged 31, the son of Israel and Mary Elizabeth Ellis of Manchester and husband of Emily Ellis of Openshaw, where he is buried in Philips Park Cemetery.

The Survivors

Flt Lt Basil Miller

Flt Lt (later Sqn Ldr) Auchinvole

F/O T B M Alexander of 109 OTU, Transport Command, Crosby on Eden.

Flt Lt John Douglas Lumsden Gammie was seriously injured and left the RAF. He was of HQ Transport Command, Bushy Park, Middlesex.

W/O G Nicholls R 1300 RCAF. There are no further details, except that he was of R Depot, Torquay, Devon

Herbert Ellis

Frank Bishop

The Visitor

Forty years later Sqn Ldr John Irvine, now a civilian, was on holiday with his wife in Oban. Relaxing for a moment on the front watching the boat trips setting out for Iona and Staffa to the accompaniment of seagull cries, they decided to go on one of the day-trips to Mull. Disembarking on the Mull side, they took the coach for a conducted tour. The coach driver, as they do, gave a running commentary on what was to be seen, pointing out things of interest and giving a brief history of the island. John Irvine was suddenly taken back to when he was Duty Cypher Officer at Reykjavik, 86 Staging Post on Iceland, where aircraft from Dorval in Canada stopped to refuel for the last lap

"There it was" said the driver "where an RAF aeroplane crashed some 2,300 feet up in the severe winter of 1945. The crash was followed by one of the most dramatic rescues of the Second World War." Sqn Ldr Irvine felt a shiver down his spine as he remembered.

That morning, in 1945, he had received a personal signal that his father had died, and was told there was a Dakota leaving the next day in which he could go to the funeral. For several weeks bad weather had hampered the air transport to Prestwick, but he did not know why he declined the offer when the next day was sunny and clear. The morning was bright and crisp as it had not been for some time and with relief they watched the Dakota take off at 11.17 hrs, setting course for Scotland. Auchinvole was a friend of his and most of the crew and passengers were known to him. The North Atlantic weather was fine, the aircraft rose to level out steadily at 10,000 ft. No doubt among the mail bags and cargo the passengers would have sat talking of their future and what they had to do before the war ended in Europe, which could not be far off now. He knew the scene only too well having been part of it so often before. Over Scotland, the weather deteriorated and night had fallen, but the pilot had made contact with Prestwick and they were all looking forward to a hot meal. John Irvine could it imagine it so clearly. Then the flight had come to an abrupt end

But now it was summer and he came back to the present, still wondering why he had declined the place on the Dakota. Who had persuaded him not to go to his own father's funeral? No one. It had just been a feeling. The next morning, back in the hotel in Oban after thinking about it all night, he wondered if the crash site still held traces of the aircraft that he had seen off that sunny day in Iceland. On returning home, he wrote to the MoD for help and was sent copies of the official reports. The map references were out of date but the British Library offered further help and translated the terms into new references.

The opportunity to visit Mull again came a few years later and this time they managed to stay in Salen, a bit nearer to his objective. Here he discussed with local people what the possibilities might be, and they, interested to hear that he had been at the start of the fatal flight told him that pieces of the aircraft had been seen and some brought down from the gorge in the mountain. It was a fine and sunny June morning when he and his wife set out on foot along Glen Forsa, the cleft between Ben Talaidh and Ben Bheag being their objective. Bogs and rivers made the going difficult but before long they were in that cleft. They both knew they were not mountaineers, so at 1000 feet he left his rucksack on a rock, knowing it would be safe. There were only deer and sheep for miles and they took no notice beyond their first curiosity.

Several times they sat down and thought of giving up. Then they saw something in the stream a little further up. A piece of metal. A few feet higher there was a heap of wreckage almost grown over with moss and lichen where the mountain stream had not reached it. Bits of engine and undercarriage, a twisted propeller, all paint gone. Was it respect for what had happened that no one had brought it down for souvenirs. It was not a war grave, all bodies had been removed, for if remains are still to be found, permission to investigate must be obtained from the MoD and the next of kin.

A moment or two of silence then a long walk back with memories of dead friends, voices across the long past intercom still heard, but now John Irvine wanted to talk to the people who had brought about the rescue. It had taken him and his wife about six hours and they felt privileged to meet those who had done it in the winter dark. Equally the rescuers were intrigued to hear the other side of the story. He told them how he had just finished his shift as Duty Cypher Officer and, on being relieved, had left the remaining signals for his replacement. Among the papers left to be transcribed was the one about his father's death.

The next day he heard of the missing aircraft he might have been on, but knew nothing of the subsequent drama.

The propeller memorial. Former RAF pilot Mac Sleven lays a wreath on behalf of Inverness branch of the Aircrew Association on 1st February 2005 following a 60th anniversary commemoration service in Salen church. The occasion was marked by a fly past from XV(R) Sqn Tornado at 12.30p.m.

TECHNICAL AND BACKGROUND

The Dakota

Dakota KK194's engines were Pratt and Whitney BP487545 port and BP488037 starboard, both listed Category B, while the aircraft itself was Category E, meaning a complete write off. The crash card for the aircraft has people inside the aircraft numbered as 3 crew, with passengers 4 and 1, Total 8. This has been altered and it is not clear, though the MoD letter lists a named 8

Originally this type of aircraft was meant to be a commercial airliner, but when WW2 came it was easily adapted to the RAF's military use. Manufactured by the American Douglas Aircraft Co, it could carry up to 28 passengers or 6,000 lbs of cargo, the equivalent of two light trucks. It had a variety of uses and could even be converted into a glider. The military version usually had a crew of three. Its main landing gear was retractable but its tail wheel was not. It could cruise comfortably at 10,000 ft at 185 mph, and was no doubt travelling at this speed when it crashed into Ben Talaidh. It could have flown higher than the summit as its ceiling was 23,000 ft and Ben Talaidh is 2,498. Why the aircraft was so low that it crashed very near the summit, can only be attributed to disorientation due to weather.

Production for this type ended in 1945 and over 13,000 had been built, many ferried over to the UK to be put to many purposes both military and civilian. It was an easy aircaft to fly and pilots liked it, except for its eccentric internal heating system. So though there is no report from the Inquiry available, no blame should be attached either to the aircraft, its crew or the system which guided it home, even though it is so suggested in the crash report. Only the weather was responsible.

Dakotas had an inadequate heating system. The crew in the cockpit could be over-warm whilst passengers in the back could be near freezing. When flying high, oxygen was needed by all if over 8 to 10 thousand feet and there were trial exercises being carried out at the time to improve its use. The oxygen system on all aircraft was recommended to be fully improved by the end of January. Whether this had been done or not in this particular Dakota we cannot know now.

There are 22 Dakotas in the U.K. still more or less complete, some still flying.

The Beaufort

Ben Talaidh is not the highest mountain on Mull. The highest, Ben More, is 3,169 feet on which a Beaufort crashed earlier in the war. The crash of the Beaufort occurred on 2nd September 1942 at 11 pm. This was a training aircraft of Bomber Command which hit the side of Ben More. Sadly, this was not an occasion for dramatic rescue, as was that of the Dakota, since all those on board were killed. All but one were Canadian – Sgt Pilot Lutes who was 24, Wireless Operator/Air Gunner Francis and the Observer Sergeant Hammond were 20. All three are buried in the Pennyfuir Cemetery outside Oban. Sergeant Hargreaves, RAF was 20 and may be buried there also though the Commonwealth War Graves Commission does not record it. They were a young crew on a navigational training flight during which there was a high increase in wind velocity and an alteration in its direction. The w/t contact failed, resulting in an error of navigation and they become lost at low altitude. The aircraft burst into flames on impact and all were killed. If there is any consolation to be had from this, it was recommended that this OTU (Operational Training Unit) improve its standards of training, which was immediately acted upon.

Carsaig

In 1941, it was planned to put a CHL (Chain Home Low) radar station at Easdale off Seil Island south of Oban, but the plan was abandoned in March of that same year in favour of Carsaig on Mull as having a longer reach over the Atlantic. It was operational by December. There were between 300 and 500 service people there, so secretly it was decided not to employ any civilians. Though they were in close touch with the navy at Tobermory and with Oban as well as with their HQ and Command, it was a lonely tour of duty. Had it not been for Mrs Gordon, whose husband was in the army and knew what it must be like, their isolation and secrecy must have been very difficult. Mrs Gordon who lived in one of the big houses, made it a home from home where all were welcome.

The station's control HQ was at Dollar in 72 Wing. This Wing had the responsibility of visiting and inspecting all the stations in its area as well as the Filter Rooms at Group HQ in Inverness, Newcastle and Belfast. It covered all the radar stations from Benbecula to the Mull of Galloway in the West and in the East, Fife to Berwick. A huge responsibility considering the ease with which U-boats could cross from occupied Norway and Denmark over the northernmost tip of Shetland and Northern Ireland into the Atlantic.

At times, American signals officers were sent to the UK to observe in 1942 how the radar system worked. One of them Lt Frank Hollandsworth, was taken on one of the inspections to Carsaig. He must have wondered to where he had come, as the road then was little more than a rough cart track as well as his having to make the bumpy crossing from Oban to Craignure in an RAF launch. At least he said it was an enjoyable ride and, during his few days stay, appreciated the beauty of the island in spite of his strange tea with the RAF of tinned herrings in tomato sauce. At Salen he stayed with the RAF inspector at Glenforsa from where he wrote that the breakfast was excellent.

In 1944, 72 Wing was absorbed into 70 Wing and as the threat to the Atlantic from German U-boats grew less, so the need for radar at Carsaig declined. Or so they thought until the Ben Talaidh tragedy of 1945. The station was put on Care and Maintenance only and the personnel gradually withdrawn and re-posted, They were sad to go. At first they had thought they were being posted to the back of beyond, though radar crews were used to that. It was like Ultima Thule, but the peace and beauty was balm to those who had gone through the Blitz of southern England and the constant threat of invasions. The Americans who came here were equally appreciative of the island's magic

Alexander MacKechnie was in the Royal Navy during the war and thinks it was the Marconi company who carried out experiments at Carsaig, though it has not been possible to verify this. He confirms that no one was allowed on or off the island without a pass and that everything at Carsaig was highly secret though the airmen were frequently seen at local dances. A building firm from Edinburgh provided a lot of work though only their own people were engaged on the secret internal installations. Great curiosity must have been aroused, but the airmen were sworn to secrecy. It is to everyone's credit, though frustrating now, even though by 1945 the radar at Carsaig had gone, nothing seems to have leaked out.

Carsaig lies on the southern edge of the island at the head of the deep bay of that name. Thus placed in relation to each other, the two stations covered the island and its western approaches. Although the searchlight facilities at Kilchiaran, on Islay, had no air role, Coast Command regarded the employment of a homing searchlight on the Isle of Man to be a matter of vital importance since their reach was long enough to guide aircraft into Prestwick. 70 and 73 Wings' searchlight equipment at Kilchiaran and Gregneish were to be operated by a crew under the directions from Port Ellen and Ramsey respectively. To work in conjunction with these, radar cover by way of a surface vessel was stationed in the Irish sea. These formed a triangular network with the installations on Mull.

Radar Hut, Carsaig

Dervaig

Dervaig lies at the head of a sea loch in north west Mull. Here was the radar CHL station. Official reports mention it only in the documents relating to other stations, there appear to be none of its own in spite of there being a large radar unit there. But strict secrecy was still essential.

A CHL – Chain Home Low Flying station – was installed primarily to detect incoming invaders in order to give early alert to other units to deal with them. These were generally set in high exposed situations, initially given numbers not names and called AMES, Air Ministry Experimental Stations. It was the sinking of the Royal Oak which alerted the defence systems to the danger from U-boats. In 1940, the installation of the first in Scotland was at Rosehearty in Aberdeenshire, a fishing village, near Fraserburgh, where there is still an air to ground weapons test range.

An RAF detachment was stationed at Dervaig living initially at the Manse, moving later into the village as their numbers increased. On the highest ground at Kilmore, above the village, an open observation post was set up, primarily to observe the movements of a solitary FW Condor which frequently appeared harrying the Atlantic convoys and taking photographs of the coastline. This aircraft and its replacements was reporting the number and position of the ships and where they were assembling to the U-boats below. The observation post reported all this back by phone to Dervaig.

Over Croig, near Dervaig, there was one spectacular engagement by a nimble RAF fighter and one of the Condors which Peter Allan MacGillivary, then a schoolboy witnessed with great excitement and recalled later for a newspaper interview.

Radar

U-boats coming from the occupied Sandinavian countries had to pass between Scotland and Iceland on their way to harass the Atlantic convoys. There were plenty of places for them to lurk, and in 1944, with the Schnorkel, their latest equipment, they were enabled to remain submerged for even longer, and come in even closer to shore to land spies and saboteurs. For a long time it seemed that they were winning, so great were the losses.

Airborne centimetric radar or ASV and similar frequency shipborne systems were the only effective means of U-boat detection other than acoustic systems such as ASDIC. The CHL system at Carsaig was for the detection of low flying aircraft. It was not to protect the base at Oban alone, but was part of the UK defence network of Radar sites. In 1941 a drum of photographs was found on a beach on western Mull. It had come from a U-boat, undamaged and was forwarded to MI5. A fascist sympathiser had provided the German Admiralty with detail charts of the west coast in this area in 1937. The police could never quite catch him although Lord Haw Haw broadcast information which clearly only he could have provided.

Material from crash of Beaufort. Display in Mull Museum, Tobermory

Notes to page 6

For the benefit of readers overseas or of non-Scottish origin, the Isle of Mull lies across the Firth of Lorn from Oban on the west coast of Scotland. To the north is its main town and war time naval base of Tobermory, from where came the stretcher bearers who carried down the casualties.

The Firth of Lorn is a continuation of Glen More, the long divide which includes Loch Ness and separates the North West Highlands from the Grampians.

When Miller was convalescent, he went to see Squadron Leader Auchinvole at Prestwick, where he tried to express his gratitude. To Sir James Ross he wrote to say how very glad he was to be alive and to tell him all this personally.

We now know from his son Alasdair, the oldest of four sons and a daughter, that Derek Auchinvole's back was broken, yet he still struggled to get down to a light far below. See the note for page 21 regarding the last exchange between Bishop and Auchinvole before the plane struck.

Note to page 8

Ben Talaidh cottage is now a bothy, kept up by the Mountain Bothy Association. In the darkness and the snow, Auchinvole had walked past it on his way to the light at Rhaoil.

Note to page 9

An account written up several years later by Dr Flora MacDonald, gives Beale and MacDonald as being amongst the third rescue party. If so, this supports the idea that they returned down the hill, once they had located the plane.

Notes to page 10

Sergeant Barnaby figures in several files of the period. He took part in a scheme to get ashore at Inchkenneth to find out about the activities of the Mitfords. Under pretence of investigating for hoarded petrol supplies, they were to search the house for radio transmitters.

The ADMI/12817 file refers to HMS Western Isles as the naval base at Tobermory was called. It had originated as a "working up" base for crews of anti-submarine vessels destined for all stations not exclusively for the Western Approaches. The Commodore was subject to the Flag-Officer for local administration and with the general operations officer of the Western Approaches Escort Forces. But, yet again, there is no mention here of the stretcher bearers who were sent out to climb Ben Talaidh.

Salen lies on the narrow neck which links the two parts of Mull at the southern end of Glen Aros on the A848. A quick look at the map shows how easy it would be to become lost on a night of bad weather, even for aircrew of Transport Command.

Notes to page 12

There were two other accidents at Prestwick within a few days of the Dakota crash, and others listed, indicating the severity of the weather and the need for continuing radar surveillance.

There are several other classes of documents at the PRO (TNA) which refer to crashes of all kinds. In none does Dakota KK194 appear. Was it meant to be a secret? Even now?

No doubt Squadron Leader R P Gillespie, the Officer commanding TAC, was very glad to welcome Auchinvole back. Here he had a light job to help his recovery and give others the benefit of his long experience. He appeared again at Prestwick, now a Squadron Leader, on 14th August 1945, apparently recovered from his ordeal. He was back at work as a Senior Control Officer after seven months.

Notes to page 13

In the records of Iceland Command Air 24/790 for that February, although there is no record of take-off, there was a three day search by four aircraft for a missing Dakota on the 6th, 7th and 8th. It was unsuccessful and they found nothing though had been expecting to find a dinghy. Whether or not this was the lost KK194, is uncertain for no number is given. If this is our Dakota, it is strange that it took five days to begin the search, by which time it was all over. The police must have informed the naval base at least in order to send the naval stretcher bearers. To whom did they pass the message?

This delay may account for the fact that Mrs Auchinvole remembered the date on which she was informed very clearly as not being the same as the date of the accident. She had reason to remember, she was in labour with their fourth child. Though the Air Ministry could not know that, it was a very insensitive time to inform her of the possible death of her husband.

The Ops Room at Reykjavik had only just re-opened on the 1st and begun to function again after a long series of bad weather. Was the coincidence of this and the date of the crash, a reason for the loss of recording a serious incident? This re-opening too may have been the cause of the delay, though surely they had been informed before the 6th by Prestwick? The four aircraft involved were from 162 RCAF, 251 and 53 Squadrons. Visibility was still bad, at times down to less than two miles in driving snow. At the same time a missing Anson had been located with one survivor.

Notes to page 15

The awards are listed in detail in the PRO (TNA) file Air 2/6952 which includes a collection of letters to and from the various people involved. There is also a page from the *London Gazette* in which their names are listed (the original meaning of the phrase "to be gazetted" comes from this inclusion). A ceremony was held in November of that year to which all were invited and the letters to each and all of these, together with many others of high rank and important reputation are also in the file, giving their addresses. Most moving of all, perhaps, are the grateful tributes paid to the islanders by the survivors.

F/O T B M Alexander of 109 OTU, came from Transport Command and was represented by Pankhurst at the ceremony.

Note to page 18
In addition, the following were personally written to by Sir James S Ross on the 14th November, from the Air Ministry

Mrs A Bishop, 11 Lofton Street, Canton, Cardiff
Mrs F Bishop, Lakeside, Ontario, Canada
Mrs H Ellis, 52 Grashan Forest, Openshaw, Manchester
Mrs N E Ellis 232 Oldham Road, Newton Heath, Manchester
Mrs Marjorie Alderton of Sunnymead, Culmington Road Sth, Croydon
WO G Nicholls RCAF R130065 R Depot Torquay, Devon
F/O Thomas M Alexander Officers' Mess, Crosby-on-Eden, Carlisle.

All these received a copy of the illuminated vellum.

Flt Lt Basil Miller wrote to Sir James Ross from No 6 Embarkation Unit, expressing his very great gratitude for everything that had been done for him, especially by Flt Lt Auchivole. He said that Ross's communication was the first he had received apart from the card he had had to complete about the recovery of his kit.

A letter in Auchinvole's small neat and very tidy script was more than appreciative of the help he had received from the islanders.

For those interested in small but important detail, there is a letter from H C Murcott, United Artists Picture Frame Manufacturers, 298 Store Street, Tottenham Court Road, London WC 1 to whom the manuscript for the text of the vellum was delivered by M C Oliver on 14 Oct 1945 at an extra cost of 10/-. Oliver was of 13 Hampstead Gardens, Golders Green NW11 and was the artist who wrote out the citation. He charged for his manuscript with the RAF badge £6 0 0. The originals of all this are at the Public Record Office, Kew, in file Air 2/6962, which is still held under restriction and must be looked at under supervision. Why, is not clear.

Notes to page 19
The main transportation of passengers between Prestwick and Dorval was VIPs of all kinds and many familiar names are recorded. There were none on this flight however, only an air traffic control officer returning to his base, the courier and the three other RAF officers. Therefore, aside from lives, it must have been an aircraft delivery flight, which was also being used, conveniently, for Air Ministry mail or something important. During 1945, 32,762 passengers were carried and 2,292,241 lbs of mail. Freight amounted to 7,475,352 lbs.

Both Oban and Tobermory police, confirmed that records are destroyed after five years, and only a few survive for London in the MEPO class of documents at the PRO (TNA). These latter seldom concern military air crashes.

All that is stated in Air 25/668 is that the Captain/pilot was F/O Bishop and he and two passengers were killed in the crash on the Isle of Mull on 1st February 1945. The curious thing is a navigator and wireless operator are not usually described as passengers, as an aircraft of this size would hardly cross the Atlantic without them. The captain of an aircraft is always the pilot, no matter what his rank of that of the others, including his crew.

Note to page 20

The names of those who did not survive are on the Index of the Commonwealth War Graves Commission at Maidenhead with the date of when and where they died, and where they are buried. There is a web site which lists their names.

Note to page 21

When he was at last able to get home Auchinvole told his wife he had gone forward into the cockpit to discuss the bad flying conditions with the pilot. He had only just returned to his seat when the aircraft struck the mountain and broke in two. This discussion in the cockpit seems to add weight to the idea of disorientation.

Notes to page 23

F/Sgt R A E Lutes was a son of Gregory William and Mary Pauline Lutes of Sault St Marie, Ontario. He is buried in Pennyfuir cemetry, Oban.
Sergeant Hargreaves R100108, son of Alfred Henry and Bertha Ann Hargreaves.
B D Francis, son of Alfred and Sara Alice of Winnipeg, Manitoba.
Sgt C Hammond 1382637.
All were of the RCAF and buried in the same Oban cemetery as Lutes. They came from the Technical Training Unit (TTU) in 17 Group, HQ at Edinburgh, and probably took off from Abbotsinch.

Notes to page 24

It was usual, if possible and the family requested it, to take the body home for burial The date of 2nd September is recorded by the CWGC though the actual accident card recording the details gives it as the 3rd and the archive at the Mull Museum says 3rd October, a month later. The latter may mean the discrepancy between the date of the crash and the burial, as CWGC cannot give total assurance as to the accuracy of their web site.

Small fragments of the Beaufort are in the Mull Museum as well as pieces of the Dakota.

Sadly, the old Glenforsa Hotel burned down on 17th December 1967.

Bibliography

Battiscombe, Stephanie, *Wren's Eye View*

Buderi, Robert, *The Invention that Changed the World* (Little, Brown & Company, 1996)

Card, Frank, *Whensoever* (Ernest Press, 1993)

Halley, James J., *Squadrons of the Royal Air Force* (Airlife)

Jones, Fred, *Air Crash*

McVicar, Don, *Ferry Command*

Nissen, Jack and Cockerill, A.W., *Winning the Radar War* (Robert Hale, 1989)

Smith, David J., *Wrecks and Relics on High Ground* (Midland publishing)

Willis Steve and Hollis Barry, *Military Airfields of the British Isles 1939-45* (Kettering, 1987)

Wilson, Eunice, *The Records of the RAF and how to find them* (FFHS, 1991)

Wilson, Eunice, *RAF Quiz Book* (Grub Street, 1993)

Wilson, Eunice, *Dangerous Sky, Resource Guide to the Battle of Britain* (Greenwood, USA, 1995)

Other books from Brown & Whittaker Publishing

Walking in North Mull
Walking in South Mull and Iona
Was it a Whale?
The Wildlife of Mull
Mull Monuments and History
Lachlan Macquarie, from Mull to Australia
A Treasure Lost – the Spanish wreck in Tobermory Bay
Traditional Tales of Mull
Glen More, a drive through history
Through the Year with St Columba, a book of prayers
Mull Family Names for Ancestor Hunters
MacLeans, a biographical dictionary
Altera Merces – graveyard inscriptions
Two Bikes and a Camera in the Highlands
A Taste of Mull
Poetry collections: Waiting for Birds, Coming to See You, Meeting the Family, Living with Mountains